Hail Mary, full of grace,

the Lord is with you!

Blessed are you among women,

and blessed is the fruit of your womb, Jesus.

Holy Mary, Mother of God,

pray for us sinners,

now and at the hour of our death.

Amen.

Revised Edition
NOW AND
AT THE HOUR OF
OUR DEATH

IMPORTANT INFORMATION CONCERNING

MY MEDICAL TREATMENT, FINANCES, DEATH AND FUNERAL

LTP

LITURGY
TRAINING
PUBLICATIONS

ACKNOWLEDGMENTS

Text by Peter Gilmour and David A. Lysik, based on a publication of Catholic Cemeteries, Archdiocese of Chicago.

This book was designed by Peter Pona, typeset in Caslon and Korinna by Jim Mellody-Pizzato, and printed by Printing Arts Chicago. The editor was David A. Lysik, and the production editor was Bryan Cones.

03 02 01 00 99   5 4 3 2 1

ISBN 1-56854-286-0
HOUR2

DISCLAIMER

Now and at the Hour of Our Death is intended to introduce the reader to several areas of concern surrounding death and dying, to invite further study, and to encourage informed decision-making. The information in this book is not intended to substitute for the advice of a trained, licensed health care or legal professional. Readers should consult their physicians as needed on questions of health care, and their attorneys for advice on legal matters.

TABLE OF CONTENTS

Death, Our Enemy and Our Friend

Nearly every person encounters death many times in the course of life. Deaths of family members, friends, associates and neighbors are intensely personal encounters with one's own mortality. Reports of other deaths — news stories, the obituaries in the daily newspaper — may not be personally involving, but they are also encounters with death for us. They remind us that everyone dies, ourselves included. Every death is a preparation for our own death.

"Life is changed, not taken away." As Christians, we believe that death is a transition, not an end. We believe that Jesus rose from the dead. We believe that dying he destroyed our death, and that rising he restored our life. We are participants in the resurrection, not spectators. This participation began with our baptism and will continue through the transition of death.

The church prays constantly for the dead and rejoices in the communion of saints. This takes place in a special way during November. The days of All Saints, November 1, and All Souls, November 2, begin this yearly reflection. As we move through November, part of our reflection is about our own death.

All our lives we pray, ". . . now and at the hour of our death." One way to give meaning to those words is to begin discussing with those concerned our wishes regarding our health care in the event we become unable to make our own decisions. Another way is to think about our own funeral and burial wishes. Other ways include planning for the management of financial resources in the event of serious illness, and considering how we wish to dispose of our possessions. When people plan well for illness and death, their plans become a gift for family and friends. Planning for serious illness and death is not solely a matter of businesslike efficiency in legal and financial matters. For Christians, planning for serious illness and death is primarily an act of stewardship and an act of faith begun in baptism.

This book is a practical guide. It gives you the opportunity to reflect on your wishes regarding your health care if you become unable to communicate your decisions. It asks you to think about what means you wish to be used to prolong your life and about such things as organ donation. It encourages you to plan in advance for the management of your financial resources and for the disposition of your goods. It allows you to record the information that your survivors will need at the time of your death.

This book also encourages you to educate yourself about the funeral industry, the options that are available for a funeral, and the costs involved. It also provides you the opportunity to think about and suggest some elements of your funeral and burial liturgy. That liturgy is the church's liturgy, the same for all the baptized regardless of wealth or attainment. But it is also intended to be a particular prayer for the individual Christian who has died.

Each November, as we pray for the dead, return to what you have written in the pages that follow. Review and update the information as needed. Daily prayer is also part of our preparation for death. The following prayer by John Henry Newman can be part of that preparation. You may wish to memorize it and pray these words every night.

> O Lord, support us all the day long,
> until the shadows lengthen,
> and the evening comes,
> and the busy world is hushed,
> and the fever of life is over,
> and our work is done.
> Then in your mercy,
> grant us a safe lodging,
> and a holy rest,
> and peace at the last.

Another beautiful text is taken from Night Prayer of the Liturgy of the Hours, which many Catholics pray every night. It recognizes that each night's sleep is a preparation for death.

> May the all-powerful Lord grant us a restful night,
> and a peaceful death.

To prepare for your own death is to make an active meditation on a great mystery. Though this book is about practical details, it also gives you a way to befriend death, to come to know little by little the meaning of the beautiful hymn that is based on a poem by Francis of Assisi:

> And you, most kind and gentle death,
> Waiting to hush our final breath,
> You lead to heaven the child of God,
> Where Christ our Lord the way has trod.

Such is the nature of life and death for those who believe that we have been raised up with Christ.

CHAPTER TWO

The Tasks surrounding Death

Many duties must be carried out and many decisions must be made at the time of death.

This chapter has two purposes. First, it gives you an overview of the tasks surrounding death. Planning for many of these tasks can be done before death, and this book provides you with the opportunity to do that in detail in the following chapters. Second, this chapter will assist your survivors as they tend to the duties and decisions that will surround your funeral and burial.

Prayers at the Time of Death

The church wishes to accompany the dying Christian with prayer. The greatest expression of this is viaticum: holy communion received by the Christian when in danger of death. When the church's minister brings the body and blood of Christ to the dying person, the minister says:

> May the Lord Jesus Christ protect you
> and lead you to eternal life.

The person who is dying responds, "Amen."

The church also gives us prayers for the moments before and following death, several of which may be found in *Catholic Household Blessings and Prayers,* available from the United States Catholic Conference, (800) 235-8722; www.nccbuscc.org. The prayers may be led by a family member, a lay minister or an ordained minister. The prayers after death are meant to be prayed before the body is removed for funeral and burial preparation. The following prayer may be used at the time of death.

> Saints of God, come to his/her aid!
> Come to meet him/her, angels of the Lord!
> Receive his/her soul and present him/her to God the Most High.

Death Certificate

In the United States, the law requires that a death certificate be issued by the county in which a person dies. The death certificate must be signed by a doctor. If the deceased has been under a doctor's care or has died in a hospital, this is a routine and expected duty of the attending physician. If the deceased has died unexpectedly, a doctor needs to be called immediately. Copies of the death certificate will be needed at a later date when filing insurance claims and probating the will, and for other legal matters.

Preparation of the Body

There are several ways in which people go about the preparation of the body for burial. The most familiar way is through the services of a funeral home. Another way is through membership in a funeral, memorial or cremation society. A third way is for people to carry out the task themselves.

While this book allows you to help and guide your survivors in their decisions at the time of your death, it does not intend to exclude family members and friends from the process of preparation for your funeral and burial. Being part of those preparations is an important way that we mourn one another. If you have attended to some details beforehand, your family may then be free to do those simple and beautiful tasks that can be a wholesome part of separation and mourning. Among these could be the washing and clothing of your body. Many funeral directors, if asked, will gladly allow family members to take part in this. Catholics affirm that the body is the temple of the Holy Spirit and insist that the body be treated with a great reverence. This reverence is not expressed in expensive coffins and lavish arrangements but in the very human tasks associated with preparing the body for burial.

Cemetery Arrangements

If you have left no plans, a representative of the cemetery will meet with your survivors and present various options. Some cemeteries limit the types and styles of grave markers according to the location of the grave and the number of graves purchased. Some require either a burial vault or a grave liner to enclose the coffin in the grave. Requirements and restrictions should be discussed before any purchase. Some cemeteries have grave sites and columbariums (places for the vessels holding ashes) set aside for cremated remains. Cremated remains may also be buried in a traditional grave.

Arrangements for the Wake and Funeral

From the perspective of faith, the rites of the church are the central actions surrounding death. Here is the sign of our faith and the consolation of those who mourn. Survivors meet with the priest or other pastoral minister from the parish of the deceased to prepare wake and funeral liturgies. Others may also give assistance to the family in preparing the liturgies and can be especially helpful by participating at the wake, funeral and burial rites.

Immediately after Burial

Many families share a meal together after the burial and extend an invitation to all who took part in the funeral liturgy. Sometimes the parish hall is used for this gathering; sometimes the family home or a hall or restaurant is used. Your survivors should know whether or not your parish is prepared to provide for such a gathering.

In the Days after Burial

It is the executor's duty to file the will in court, usually within 30 days of death. If no will exists, survivors will need to consult an attorney to determine the proper procedure to be followed.

A provision in most wills gives the executor power to pay funeral and burial costs from the estate of the deceased. If no previous arrangement has been made, survivors need to work with the executor of the will to purchase an appropriate burial marker if one is desired.

CHAPTER THREE

Preparation of the Body

The church's *Order of Christian Funerals* says this of the preparation of the body:

> Since in baptism the body was marked with the seal of the Trinity and became the temple of the Holy Spirit, Christians respect and honor the bodies of the dead and the places where they rest. Any customs associated with the preparation of the body of the deceased should always be marked with dignity and reverence and never with the despair of those who have no hope. Preparation of the body should include prayer, especially in those intimate moments reserved for family members. For the final disposition of the body, it is the ancient Christian custom to bury or entomb the bodies of the dead; cremation is permitted, unless it is evident that cremation was chosen for anti-Christian motives.
>
> In countries or regions where an undertaker, and not the family or community, carries out the preparation and the transfer of the body, the pastor and other ministers are to ensure that the undertakers appreciate the values and beliefs of the Christian community.
>
> The family and friends of the deceased should not be excluded from taking part in the services sometimes provided by undertakers, for example, the preparation and laying out of the body.

These words may help to guide the various decisions to be made about preparation of the body.

Funeral Home

If the services of a funeral home are to be employed, some planning can be done in advance. If you have made no advance plans, your survivors will need to tend to a variety of things — making choices about burial, entombment and cremation, selecting the coffin or a vessel for cremated remains, deciding questions of embalming and visitation, and dealing with costs and financial concerns — often without adequate time and while simultaneously dealing with the range of emotions that accompany a death. Your survivors will also need to arrange the time of the wake, funeral liturgy and committal at the cemetery with the parish church. Finally, they will need to notify others of your death, and make a decision regarding the presence and content of an obituary notice in the newspapers.

The vast majority of people in the United States choose a funeral home to assist them at the time of death. Two practical considerations should guide you in the choice of a funeral home. The first is its reputation. Are people who have used a specific funeral home willing to recommend it? The second is cost. Use the following information to guide you in your efforts to make good decisions about planning for your funeral.

GATHERING INFORMATION • You should first be aware that when you arrange for a funeral, you have the option of purchasing a package of items and services, or of buying individual items and services to meet your own needs. You need only select and pay for those goods and services that you want.

A federal regulation known as the Funeral Rule, enacted by the Federal Trade Commission (FTC), requires funeral homes (but not cemeteries) to provide you with certain information, whether you shop by phone or in person. Under the Funeral Rule, if you contact a funeral home by telephone and ask about funeral arrangements you must be given the prices of the services you ask about. If you contact a funeral home in person, you must be given a written copy of an itemized price list that gives the cost of each service offered by the funeral home. The Funeral Rule also requires the funeral home to provide written price lists for coffins (caskets) and for outer burial containers (vaults or grave liners).

More detailed information about the Funeral Rule may be found in the FTC publication, *Funerals: A Consumer Guide,* available from the Consumer Response Center, Federal Trade Commission, Washington DC 20580; (202) 326-2222; the FTC website www.ftc.gov; the Consumer Information Center website www.pueblo.gsa.gov; or from the Consumer Information Center, P. O. Box 100, Pueblo CO 81002; (888) 878-3256. Also available from the FTC is the publication *Caskets and Burial Vaults,* which provides an overview of the Funeral Rule as it relates specifically to these products.

Use the Funeral Rule to help you gather information about your options for funeral and burial arrangements. Consider visiting at least two or three funeral homes (perhaps with a spouse or friend) to obtain their price lists for services, coffins and outer burial containers. Comparing lists of services and products you think you would want will give you an idea of how much your funeral might cost. You can use these lists to help form your own preferences. They might also help you to rethink your wishes in light of the costs. Use this information to prepare a brief statement about what you consider important features of your funeral and burial.

PREPAYING FOR FUNERAL GOODS AND SERVICES • Learning about funeral costs in advance of your death can also help you begin to form plans to meet those costs. In the vast majority of cases, the pitfalls and risks of prepaying for funeral goods and services probably outweigh the benefits. Consider instead the simple option of opening a funeral savings account at a bank that will be payable to your next of kin upon your death (a Totten trust). Designate the account "payable on death," and deposit funds sufficient to meet your wishes; the accrued interest will help counter the effects of inflation.

In the event you decide to prepay for your funeral arrangements, do so with your eyes open and be sure to ask many questions before agreeing to any contract. Clear up any misunderstandings before paying, and be sure to receive a written description of what goods and services are included. State laws vary regarding the handling of the money you prepay, and you should learn your state's law if you are prepaying.

Ideally, you will want 100% of the amount you prepay for funeral goods and services to be held in trust, with the interest income deposited in the trust fund account. You should receive an annual report regarding your trust fund. You will also want to avoid what is called the "constructive delivery" of your prepaid, pre-need funeral goods, that is, the legal fiction that when you receive a statement of purchase and ownership of your pre-need funeral goods, you are deemed to have "taken delivery" of them even if you have not really done so (that is, have not yet used the coffin, urn or grave marker). Constructive delivery allows the funeral home or cemetery immediate access to your funds — even those intended by you to be held in trust — and effectively operates to frustrate any claim you may make for a refund in the event you change your plans. You will want the right to cancel any pre-need purchase on written notice, and receive a full refund including interest. Alternatively, you will want to be able to transfer the trust fund, without paying a fee, to another funeral home in the event that you relocate, die away from your home, or change your plans. For more consumer information, contact the American Association of Retired Persons, 601 E Street NW, Washington DC 20049; www.aarp.org; or consult *Caring for the Dead: Your Final Act of Love,* by Lisa Carlson (Hinesburg, Vermont: Upper Access Books, 1998), available from Upper Access Books, P. O. Box 457, Hinesburg VT 05461; (800) 356-9315; (802) 482-2988; www.upperaccess.com.

As your plans begin to take shape, be sure to let your family members and loved ones know of your decisions. Keep copies of any paperwork in a place that is secure yet readily accessible to your survivors. Use what you learn about your options for funeral services and goods to make choices and plans that reflect your values and your faith.

☐　I have visited two or three funeral homes and collected their price lists.

☐　I have set up a funeral savings account (a Totten trust) at the
following bank:
Name of bank _____
Address_____

_____

Account number _____
Payable to_____

☐　I have decided not set up a funeral savings account.

☐ I have prepaid for funeral arrangements with this funeral home:

Name_____

Address_____

_____

Telephone_____

Contact person_____

The contract is kept_____

The contract includes the following:

☐ provision that 100% of money prepaid be held in a trust account

☐ provision that interest earned be deposited in the account

☐ provision that the agreement may be canceled at any time upon written notice, with a full refund; or that funds may be transferred without fee to another funeral home

☐ the following provisions that my survivors should be aware of:

_____

_____

_____

_____

_____

_____

☐ I have decided not to prepay for funeral arrangements. I suggest the following arrangements:

_____

_____

_____

_____

_____

_____

Memorial Society

Memorial societies advocate simple burial practices at economical costs. They function like consumer organizations. A memorial society's role is advisory and sometimes contractual. Members are provided with information about economical funeral and burial arrangements. Some societies have contractual arrangements with specified funeral homes; these homes agree to provide adequate services at predetermined prices. The Funeral and Memorial Societies of America (FAMSA) is a good source of information: Call (800) 765-1017, or visit their website www.funerals.org/famsa. The book, *The American Way of Death Revisited,* by Jessica Mitford (New York: Alfred A. Knopf, 1998), contains an extensive listing of not-for-profit funeral and memorial societies in the United States and Canada.

☐   I have a membership in the following memorial society:

Name_____

Address_____

_____

Telephone_____

Contact person_____

Specific arrangements of my membership:

_____

_____

_____

_____

_____

_____

Private Burial

Some people choose to bury their own dead. People who take this option should know the local legislation that governs the disposal of bodies, and they must be able to carry out the tasks of private burial. *Caring for the Dead: Your Final Act of Love,* by Lisa Carlson (Hinesburg, Vermont: Upper Access Books, 1998), provides valuable information on this subject and includes state-by-state funeral law materials for the consumer. The book is available from Upper Access Books, P. O. Box 457, Hinesburg VT 05461; (800) 356-9315; (802) 482-2988; www.upperaccess.com; and from the FAMSA website www.funerals.org/famsa.

☐   I wish to be buried without the assistance of a funeral home or memorial society. I have investigated this fully and have made the following arrangements with my family and friends:

_____

_____

_____

_____

_____

_____

The Coffin

Robert Hovda has written of the coffin in this way:

> The container for the dead body of a believer should be honestly that, and beautiful as simple and well-crafted things are beautiful. The liturgical books of the church tell us that "any kind of pomp or display should be avoided." . . . The dead body as the sign of the person is what demands honor and reverence, not the coffin. The coffin is the container whose only purpose is to frame and transport the body. There are times in life for

festival excess, but this moment is too sacred for that. It is a reflective moment of truth and of farewell, so it wants and demands sturdy, honest, straightforward, basic talk and action and objects. One's death or the death of a loved one is too fundamentally important for make-believe and tinsel, or for simulating the bedroom or the couch. ("The Amen Corner," *Worship* 59, page 258).

The coffin or casket is often the single most expensive item in a traditional funeral. In 1996, the average price for low- to mid-priced coffins was over $1,600. On your visits to funeral homes be sure to obtain coffin price lists for comparison. However, coffins themselves may be purchased from sources other than a funeral home, and you might find it productive to research other providers. The obituary pages of newspapers often contain advertisements by coffin retailers, and many coffin creators, woodworkers and retailers maintain websites that can be located after a simple search. In addition, the website www.casketstores.com/Directory.htm provides links to several casket retail outlets that maintain online showrooms and price lists. This website might be another place to consult for initial comparison shopping.

If you wish to be cremated, there are some additional concerns that you should be aware of. If a coffin is desired, it must be one that is suitable for cremation — generally, one that is made of solid wood or a cloth-covered wood composite. However, a coffin is not required for cremation, and all funeral homes must provide what the federal Funeral Rule calls "alternative containers," heavy cardboard containers intended to be used for cremation. These alternative containers provide a certain economy over coffins when cremation is desired. However, in order to balance economy with a desire to maintain dignity at the celebration of funeral rites where the body is to be present, you may wish to ask the funeral homes you visit about leasing an attractive coffin for viewing and funeral rites, and purchasing an alternative container for cremation.

☐   I have made the following arrangements for a coffin:

_____

_____

_____

_____

_____

_____

☐   I have not made arrangements for a coffin. These are my wishes:

_____

_____

_____

_____

_____

_____

☐   I have made other arrangements as follows:

_____

_____

_____

_____

_____

Burial and Cremation

While there are several options for the disposition of the body, the Christian community always marks the moment with prayer. The church's funeral rite provides that the place of committal is blessed as a place of honor in expectation of the glory of the resurrection.

> God of endless ages,
> through disobedience to your law we fell from grace
> and death entered the world;
> but through the obedience and resurrection of your Son
> you revealed to us a new life.
> You granted Abraham, our father in faith,
> a burial place in the promised land;
> you prompted Joseph of Arimathea
> to offer his own tomb for the burial of the Lord.
> In a spirit of repentance we earnestly ask you
> to look upon this grave [*or* tomb, *or* place] and bless it,
> so that, while we commit to the earth [*or* to its resting place]
> the body [*or* earthly remains] of your servant [name]
> his/her soul may be taken into paradise.

Burial Arrangements

Larger cemeteries offer many options for location, family plots, memorial markers, above-ground entombment in mausoleums and placement of cremated remains. Some of the costs associated with the cemetery can include the price of the lot, burial vault or grave liner (if required by the cemetery), vault or liner installation charge, opening and closing charges (typically higher on weekends), marker installation charge and the cemetery "counselor's" commission.

Markers themselves may be purchased from sources other than the cemetery. Local newspaper obituary pages often have advertisements from companies that provide markers for retail sale. Many cemeteries require either a burial vault or a grave liner into which the coffin is placed. The vault or liner is typically made of reinforced concrete and is meant to prevent the ground from sinking as the coffin deteriorates.

As with funeral home goods and services, you may choose to prepay for your cemetery goods and services. Again, be sure that your decision to do so is an informed one. Gather price lists from two or three cemeteries. Use the information you gather to prepare a brief statement about what you consider important features of your burial.

In many locations throughout the country, cemeteries have on-site funeral homes that are either owned by the cemetery or are contracted by the cemetery to operate on cemetery property. Do not assume that the combination funeral home-cemetery will automatically be the best choice for all your needs.

If you decide to prepay for your burial arrangements, be sure to receive a written statement of what goods and services are included. As with the pre-need purchase of funeral goods and services, you will want 100% of the amount you prepay for burial goods and services (not including the cost of the lot, crypt or niche) to be held in trust, with interest to be deposited in the account. You will want to avoid "constructive delivery" (see page 12 for more on this), and will want the right to cancel your pre-need purchases on written notice and receive a full refund if your needs or desires change over time. Alternatively, you will want to be able to transfer the trust funds to another cemetery. Additionally, you will want to be able to sell your unused lot, crypt or niche back to the cemetery if your plans change. In this case, you will want to check the prices of comparable properties to determine a fair resale price, especially if several years have elapsed since the time of purchase.

Veterans should be aware that they, their spouses and their dependent children are entitled to burial without cost in a national cemetery.

☐ I have decided to prepay for my burial arrangements:

Name of cemetery_____

Location of cemetery_____

_____

Contact person_____

Name of lot or crypt holder_____

Easement or deed number_____

Legal description of graves or crypts as shown on easement or deed:

_____

_____

_____

_____

Other burial goods or services_____

_____

The contract is kept_____

The contract includes the following:

☐ provision that 100% of money prepaid for burial goods and services be held in a trust account

☐ provision that interest earned be deposited in the account

☐ provision that the agreement may be canceled at any time upon written notice, with a full refund; or that funds may be transferred without fee to another cemetery

☐ provision that the cemetery buy back unused lot, crypt or niche if plans change

☐ the following provisions that my survivors should be aware of:

_____

_____

_____

_____

☐ I am a lot holder and have made arrangement with the cemetery to assign graves to specific individuals. The arrangements are:

Grave number   *Assigned to*

_____

_____

_____

☐ I have decided not to prepay for burial goods and services. I suggest the following:

_____

_____

_____

_____

_____

Cremation

Cremation, the practice of burning the body of a deceased person, may be a confusing issue for Catholics. At one time the church prohibited cremation, except in cases of natural disaster or plague, because it was seen as a denial of the resurrection and an offense against traditional Christian reverence for the body. This is no longer the case and the church allows cremation for any sound reason.

The 1997 document of the United States Bishops' Committee on the Liturgy, *Reflections on the Body, Cremation, and Catholic Funeral Rites*, observes:

> The long-standing practice of burying the body of the deceased in a grave or tomb in imitation of the burial of Jesus' body continues to be encouraged as a sign of Christian faith. However, owing to contemporary cultural interaction, the practice of cremation has become part of Catholic practice in the United States and other parts of the Western world. . . .
>
> In certain states cremation of the body is used in more than 40 percent of all funerals. In general, cremation is used in 20 percent of all funerals in the United States. . . .
>
> While promoting the values that underlie our preference for burial of the body, we must exercise sensitive pastoral judgment concerning the choice that nearly 20 percent of our people are making in favor of cremation. Economic, geographic, ecological, or family factors on occasion make the cremation of a body the only feasible choice.

Regarding the treatment of the cremated remains of a body, the *Order of Christian Funerals* states:

> The cremated remains of a body should be treated with the same respect given to the human body from which they come. This includes the use of a worthy vessel to contain the ashes, the manner in which they are carried, the care and attention to appropriate placement and transport, and the final disposition. The cremated remains should be buried in a grave or entombed in a mausoleum or columbarium. The practice of scattering

cremated remains on the sea, from the air, or on the ground, or keeping cremated remains in the home of a relative or friend of the deceased are not the reverent disposition that the church requires. Whenever possible, appropriate means for recording with dignity the memory of the deceased should be adopted, such as a plaque or stone which records the name of the deceased.

Cremation arrangements are most commonly made either through a funeral home or through membership in a cremation society. As with funeral and cemetery goods and services, you may choose to prepay for your cremation goods and services. Cremation societies often advertise on the obituary pages of local newspapers, and you should contact as many as possible to obtain product and price lists for comparison. If prepaying for cremation services, you will want 100% of the amount you prepay to be held in trust, with interest deposited in the account, and the right to cancel and receive a full refund including interest.

There are many different options for the timing of cremation. For example, you may arrange for direct cremation without embalming upon death, before any funeral liturgy. In this case, the cremated remains may be brought to church for the funeral Mass. Or you may arrange for the funeral rites to be celebrated in the presence of the body, with cremation following the funeral Mass. (See page 17 for information on the use of a coffin in this case.) Not every funeral home or cremation society offers every option, and you may need to contact several cremation service providers to find one that will meet your needs.

☐ I wish to be cremated and have made these arrangements:

_____

_____

_____

_____

_____

☐ I wish to be cremated, but have made no arrangements.

☐ I have made these arrangements for the disposition of my cremated remains:

_____

_____

_____

_____

_____

☐ I have made no arrangements for the disposition of my cremated remains, but ask the following:

_____

_____

_____

_____

_____

_____

Memorial Marker and Inscription

☐ I have arrangements for a memorial marker with the following company or organization:

Name_____

Address_____

_____

Telephone_____

Contact person_____

The arrangements are:

_____

_____

_____

_____

☐ I do not have arrangements for a memorial marker. I would prefer the following (check first with the cemetery for specific regulations):

_____

_____

_____

_____

You may wish to suggest a particular religious symbol or text on a memorial marker.

Inscribe my name as:

_____

Suggested religious symbol, if any:

_____

Suggested words, if any:

_____

The Order of Christian Funerals

The rituals and prayers surrounding death are a witness to the faith of the one who has died. They give comfort to the community of family, friends and associates who have surrounded the dead person during life. These rituals affirm and express solidarity between the living and the dead in the communion of saints.

Approach these rituals and prayers as one prayer, like a procession that moves from the deathbed to the place of committal. Within this procession there are some moments that we mark by gathering to pray either around the body of the deceased or in the presence of the cremated remains of the body. In the *Order of Christian Funerals*, the Catholic book of services for death and burial, these special moments are the vigil or wake service, the funeral liturgy itself, and the burial.

When the choice has been made to cremate a body, the *Order of Christian Funerals* prefers that the body of the deceased be present for the various funeral rites, and that cremation follow the funeral Mass. However, when cremation takes place shortly after death, it is appropriate that the cremated remains of the body be present during the vigil service and the funeral liturgy.

The Vigil or Wake

This is the principal time of prayer before the funeral liturgy itself. It is usually celebrated by an assembly of family members and friends. The vigil may take place in the home of the deceased, at the funeral home, or at the church (if the body or the cremated remains are brought to the church well before the funeral liturgy). In the United States, the vigil is most commonly celebrated in the funeral home.

The *Order of Christian Funerals* offers two models for the vigil. The first is a liturgy of the word. Everyone present is encouraged to take part by prayers and intercessions, by listening to the word of God, by joining in psalms and song. A minister from the parish usually presides at the wake service and a leader of song is often present.

This liturgy begins with song and prayer. Then there are usually two readings from scripture, with the second of these taken from the one of the gospels. A psalm is prayed between the two readings and a short homily may follow the gospel. There are then prayers of intercession, the Lord's Prayer and a concluding prayer and blessing. The vigil ends with all joining in song. When cremation has taken place before the vigil, the prayers are adapted as necessary; in this case the final commendation and the committal may also be celebrated at the vigil.

It is appropriate that during this vigil service some family members and friends speak in memory of the deceased. This can be an informal sharing of memories. Often the service brings together persons who have known the deceased at various times or in a variety of settings. Together they can share a larger memory than any single person has alone.

From the list of scripture readings on pages 37 – 39, you may wish to select several options from which your family can choose the readings for your vigil service:

_____

_____

_____

_____

_____

You may also wish to suggest one or two persons who could begin the time of sharing memories:

_____

_____

The *Order of Christian Funerals* offers a second model for the vigil — Morning Prayer or Evening Prayer. While these forms of prayer are largely unfamiliar to most people, if your parish has experience with Morning or Evening Prayer, you might wish to consider it for your wake service.

Other Prayers

The church prays not only at the time of the vigil or wake service, but at the deathbed, at the first viewing of the body, and when the body or cremated remains are moved to the church or place of committal.

At the Time of Death • Family, ministers and others from the Christian community are, if possible, present when death takes place. In the last moments of life, they commend the dying person to the Lord. Their prayer continues after death while still in the presence of the body:

Almighty God and Father,
by the mystery of the cross, you have made us strong;
by the sacrament of the resurrection
you have sealed us as your own.
Look kindly upon your servant [name],
now freed from the bonds of mortality,
and count him/her among your saints in heaven.
We ask this through Christ our Lord.

The leader may also lead a prayer for the mourners:

Father of mercies and God of all consolation,
you pursue us with untiring love
and dispel the shadow of death
with the bright dawn of life.
Comfort your family in their loss and sorrow.
Be our refuge and our strength, O Lord,
and lift us from the depths of grief
into the peace and light of your presence.

GATHERING IN THE PRESENCE OF THE BODY • Prayer is appropriate
when family members and friends first gather in the presence of the
body—to prepare it for burial or to view the body after others have prepared it. Someone from the parish community may be present to lead
a simple service of prayer that can include these words from the Gospel
of Matthew:

Come to me, all you who labor and are burdened,
and I will give you rest.
Take my yoke upon you and learn from me,
for I am meek and humble of heart;
and you will find rest for yourselves.
For my yoke is easy, and my burden light.

The body may be sprinkled with holy water as a reminder of baptism. Then a psalm and the Lord's Prayer are prayed by all. The leader then prays that the one who has died be welcomed into paradise "where there will be no more sorrow, no weeping nor pain, but the fullness of peace and joy." If this first gathering takes place after the body has been cremated, the prayers are adapted as needed.

TRANSFER OF THE BODY OR CREMATED REMAINS TO THE CHURCH OR PLACE OF COMMITTAL • The Catholic *Order of Christian Funerals* also provides a rite for use "with the family and close friends as they prepare to accompany the body of the deceased to the church or to the place of committal." This short rite includes an invitation to prayer, a short scripture verse, a litany, the Lord's Prayer and a concluding prayer. It is to be adapted when the cremated remains of the body are present. This time of prayer ends with the invitation to those present to proceed with the body or the vessel containing the cremated remains to the church or place of committal:

> The Lord guards our coming in and our going out.
> May God be with us today
> as we make this last journey with our brother/sister.

While in practice this brief rite has been ignored, there is no reason that it cannot be part of the prayer of the family members and close friends who accompany the body or the cremated remains of the deceased from the funeral home to the church.

The Funeral Liturgy

The funeral liturgy is the central moment in the procession from death to burial. The body, or the vessel containing the cremated remains, is usually brought to the parish church. The funeral liturgy includes the formal reception of the body or cremated remains, the liturgy of the word, the liturgy of the eucharist and the final commendation.

THE FORMAL RECEPTION OF THE BODY OR CREMATED REMAINS • The church's minister, in the name of the whole community, greets the mourners and sprinkles the coffin or the vessel containing the cremated remains with holy water. If a coffin is used, it is then covered with a pall. These gestures call to mind baptism, in which the deceased person died to sin and put on the Lord Jesus Christ. The pall, which is the same simple fabric no matter who is being buried, reminds us that the baptized are brothers and sisters, all the world's distinctions put aside. The assembled people then join in song as the coffin or the vessel containing the cremated remains is carried into the church; the mourners follow and go to their places.

THE LITURGY OF THE WORD • Two or three passages from scripture are then read, the last of which is taken from one of the gospels. A brief homily follows and then all join in prayers of intercession.

THE LITURGY OF THE EUCHARIST • The eucharist is celebrated with the bringing of bread and wine to the altar, the eucharistic prayer and the communion rite. The liturgy of the eucharist is omitted on days when a funeral Mass is not to be celebrated (namely, days of obligation, Holy Thursday, Good Friday, Holy Saturday, the Sundays of Advent, Lent and the Easter season), when a priest is not available, or when for good reasons the pastor and family decide that a liturgy without the eucharist is the more suitable form of celebration.

FINAL COMMENDATION • This is the solemn farewell in which the community entrusts the deceased to the merciful embrace of God. After the final commendation, the family and some members of the community usually go in procession to the place of burial. If the body is to be cremated, arrangements are sometimes made for those who wish to do so to accompany the body to the place of cremation.

From the list of scripture readings on pages 37 – 39, you may wish to suggest one or several from which your family can choose to be read at your funeral. You may also wish to note why you have chosen a specific reading. The readings at the funeral liturgy should be different than those at the wake service. The final reading is always from the gospel.

_____

_____

_____

_____

_____

_____

In the prayers of intercession, the church prays for its own needs, for the needs of the world and especially for the poor. We pray also for the specific needs of the community that has gathered for this funeral. If there are certain petitions you wish to have made at your funeral, list them here.

_____

_____

_____

_____

_____

_____

Most of the music for the funeral liturgy is taken from the music that is sung at Sunday Mass at the parish. The processional songs will be chosen for their appropriateness to Christian death and burial. You may wish to make suggestions for songs that would be appropriate.

_____

_____

_____

Various ministries are needed at every liturgy. Family members or friends may perform some of these ministries at funerals. You may wish to make suggestions below.

Two or more persons may place the pall over the coffin. The pall is a reminder of the garment we were given at baptism when we were clothed with Christ.

_____

_____

Usually one or two parish lectors or the presiding minister will proclaim the reading(s) before the gospel, unless family members or friends are able to do this.

_____

_____

Members of the family or friends may bring up the bread and wine at the beginning of the liturgy of the eucharist.

_____

_____

Both women and men may be pallbearers. Honorary pallbearers may also be named.

Other persons may be suggested to serve as ushers, altar servers and ministers of the eucharist.

A member of the family or a friend may speak in remembrance of the deceased before the final commendation.

The Committal

The committal is the final ritual in the movement from death to burial. It is celebrated at the grave or crematorium or wherever interment is to take place. The living commit the dead to the earth, tomb or fire, but in reality they commit the dead to the love of God to await the glory of the resurrection:

> In sure and certain hope of the resurrection to eternal life
> through our Lord Jesus Christ,
> we commend to Almighty God our brother/sister [name],

and we commit his/her body [*or* earthly remains] to the ground
   [*or* the deep *or* the elements *or* its resting place]:
[earth to earth,] ashes to ashes, dust to dust.
The Lord bless him/her and keep him/her,
the Lord make his face to shine upon him/her
   and be gracious to him/her,
the Lord lift up his countenance upon him/her
   and give him/her peace.

The final prayer repeats our hope:

God of the living and the dead,
accept our prayers
for those who have died in Christ
[and are buried with him in the hope of rising again].
Since they were true to your name on earth,
let them praise you for ever in the joy of heaven.

The last words of the rite are words of blessing for the living:

May the peace of God,
which is beyond all understanding,
keep your hearts and minds
in the knowledge and love of God
and of his Son, our Lord Jesus Christ.

If the body is to be cremated, a subsequent gathering with prayer at the time of the burial or entombment of the cremated remains is appropriate.

If you would like the committal to take place at the side of the grave, or if you would like the coffin or the vessel containing the cremated remains to be placed in the grave while the mourners are present, or if you have other specific requests, you may enter them here. In most places, the family must make these requests known to the cemetery before the funeral and be prepared to deal with possible restrictions (and perhaps extra cost) imposed by the cemetery.

Scripture Readings for Wake and Funeral Liturgies

The scripture readings listed here are those provided in the *Order of Christian Funerals*. The single line with each is intended to summarize one thought from each reading. Rather than depend on these summary lines, it would be best to read each text in its entirety.

Hebrew Scripture Readings

Job 19:1, 23 – 27
I know that my Redeemer lives.

Wisdom 3:1 – 9
He accepted them as a holocaust.

Wisdom 4:7–15
A blameless life is a ripe old age.

Isaiah 25:6a, 7 – 9
The Lord will prepare a feast and wipe away the tears from every face.

Lamentations 3:17– 26
It is good to wait in silence for the Lord God to save.

Daniel 12:1 – 3
Many of those who sleep in the dust of the earth shall awake.

2 Maccabees 12:43 – 46
It is good and holy to think of the dead rising again.

New Testament Readings

Acts of the Apostles 10:34 – 43
God has appointed Jesus as judge of the living and the dead.

Romans 5:5 – 11
Since we are now justified by Christ's blood, we will be saved through him.

Romans 5:17 – 21
When sin increased, there grace abounded all the more.

Romans 6:3 – 9
Let us walk in newness of life.

Romans 8:14 – 23
We groan within ourselves as we wait for adoption, the redemption of our bodies.

Romans 8:31b – 35, 37 – 39
If God is for us, who can be against us?

Romans 14:7 – 9, 10b – 12
Whether we live or die, we belong to the Lord.

1 Corinthians 15:20 – 23, 24b – 28
In Christ all people shall be brought to life.

1 Corinthians 15:51 – 57
Death is swallowed up in victory.

2 Corinthians 4:14 — 5:1
What is seen is transitory, but what is unseen is eternal.

2 Corinthians 5:1, 6 – 10
We have an everlasting home in heaven.

Philippians 3:20 – 21
Jesus will change our lowly bodies to conform with his glorified body.

1 Thessalonians 4:13 – 18
We shall stay with the Lord for ever.

2 Timothy 2:8 – 13
If we have died with Christ, we shall also live with Christ.

1 John 3:1 – 2
We shall see God.

1 John 3:14 – 16
We have passed from death to life, because we love our brothers and sisters.

Revelation 14:13
Happy are those who die in the Lord.

Revelation 20:11 — 21:1
The dead have been judged according to their works.

Revelation 21:1 – 5a, 6b – 7
There shall be no more death or mourning.

Gospel Readings

Matthew 5:1–12a
Rejoice and be glad, for your reward will be great in heaven.

Matthew 11:25–30
Come to me and I will give you rest.

Matthew 25:1–13
Behold, the bridegroom! Come out to meet him!

Matthew 25:31–46
Come, you who are blessed by my Father.

Mark 15:33–39, 16:1–6
Jesus gave a loud cry and breathed his last.

Luke 7:11–17
Young man, I tell you, arise!

Luke 12:35–40
You must be prepared.

Luke 23:33, 39–43
Today you will be with me in paradise.

Luke 23:44–46, 50, 52–53; 24:1–6a
Father, I put my life in your hands.

Luke 24:13–35
Was it not necessary that the Christ should suffer and so enter into his glory?

John 5:24–29
Whoever hears my word and believes, has passed from death to life.

John 6:37–40
All who believe in the Son will have eternal life and I will raise them to life again on the last day.

John 6:51–58
Whoever eats this bread will live for ever; and I will raise them on the last day.

John 11:17–27
I am the resurrection and the life.

John 11:32–45
Lazarus, come out!

John 12:23–28
If a grain of wheat falls to the ground and dies, it produces much fruit.

John 14:1–6
In my Father's house there are many dwelling places.

John 17:24–26
Father, I want those you have given me to be with me where I am.

John 19:17–18, 25–30
Jesus bowed his head and gave up his spirit.

CHAPTER SIX

Obituary, Death Notice and Memorial Card Information

Obituaries and death notices include information about one's life and family. By filling out the following pages carefully and completely, you will leave these needed records.

Biographical Information

Full name_____

Name before marriage_____

Date of birth_____ Place of birth_____

Baptism (church, location, date)_____

_____

Married to_____

Place and date of marriage_____

_____

Previous marriages_____

_____

Parents:

Name	Place of residence	Date of birth/death

Children:

Name	Place of residence	Date of birth/death

Grandparents:

Name	Place of residence

Grandchildren and great-grandchildren:

Name	Parents

Brothers and sisters, other relatives:

Name   *Relationship*

_____

_____

_____

_____

_____

_____

_____

_____

Education:

School   *Location*   *Dates*   *Diploma/Degree*

_____

_____

_____

_____

Military service:

Branch of service_____

Serial number_____

Dates of service and rank_____

Veterans Affairs claim number_____

Death benefits:

_____

_____

_____

Location of discharge papers_____

Work history:

Position   *Location*   *Dates*

_____

_____

_____

_____

_____

_____

_____

Union membership:

_____

_____

Social Security number_____

Previous residences:

Address or city   *Dates*

_____

_____

_____

_____

_____

_____

_____

_____

_____

_____

_____

Accomplishments and honors:

_____

_____

_____

_____

Memorial Card

In many places it is customary to have memorial cards that list the name, dates of birth and death, and sometimes other information about the deceased. These cards often have religious images and texts from scripture or prayers. Funeral homes may offer a selection of such cards with an image and prayer already printed on them, but the family may choose to have a simple card prepared and printed before the wake and funeral.

You may wish to specify a particular scriptural text or prayer for your memorial card.

_____

_____

_____

_____

_____

Is there anything else that might be appropriate on this card?

_____

_____

_____

Memorial Requests

Flowers and contributions to charities are customary memorials given by family and friends at the time of death. Many people prefer to give specific memorials in accordance with the wishes of the deceased. These wishes are usually printed in the obituary and death notices. Indicate any special preference for memorials.

_____

_____

_____

_____

_____

_____

Persons to Notify

If there are persons who should be notified of your death, especially those unlikely to see a death notice or those not well known by your immediate family, you can list them here.

Name   *Telephone*

_____

_____

_____

_____

_____

_____

_____

_____

Legal Information

We live in a complex society, and the legalities surrounding death may seem cumbersome. Leaving a will and furnishing information about insurance and death benefits is a great kindness to your survivors. The time and expense involved need not be great.

Medical knowledge now makes it possible to prolong life to an extent that, in individual cases, may be neither necessary nor wise nor compassionate. Legal concerns surround medical practices. When the time comes for decisions, you may be incapable of communicating your own wishes regarding prolonged treatment. That is why many people now give clear direction to both medical personnel and family members regarding their wishes about prolonging life in exceptional circumstances.

Advances in medicine also make it possible for people to donate their organs for specific uses or their bodies for medical research. Such decisions should be made well in advance of death.

Family members should be informed of decisions regarding prolonged medical treatment and donation of organs or of the body. Cards indicating such decisions should be carried.

Making a Will

A will is a legal document, usually drawn up by a lawyer and witnessed by at least two people. If you care about how your financial and material assets are distributed after your death, you need a will. Even if you consider yourself to be of modest financial means, or if you have set up certain direct beneficiary transfers (contracts such as life insurance policies, IRAs, trust accounts, and so on, where the assets are distributed apart from a will) or a living trust, it is a good idea to consider making a will.

A will lets you control how your estate will be distributed, and thus gives you the opportunity to make the best arrangements for those you care about. In your will you can also name a guardian for young children. If you die intestate (that is, without a will), any property that has not been distributed by other means will be distributed according to state intestacy laws, under which only spouses and blood relatives may inherit; friends, domestic partners and charities may not inherit under state intestacy laws.

While individuals with large estates should definitely consult an attorney when preparing a will, it is prudent for anyone considering a will to work with an attorney. In many larger cities, local bar associations sponsor programs that offer no- or low-cost will-related consultation with an attorney and low-cost preparation of a simple will. In addition, bar associations also provide lawyer referral services. A free informative pamphlet entitled *Making a Will* is available from the Consumer Information Center, P. O. Box 100, Pueblo CO 81002; (888) 878-3256; www.pueblo.gsa.gov.

In your will you will need to appoint an executor—a person responsible for carrying out the directions in your will. This person should be someone who is trustworthy, competent to handle financial matters, able to communicate clearly, and someone with whom you feel close enough to share a wide range of personal facts. In some situations, it might be beneficial to discuss the appointment of your executor with your family members. Contact the above-mentioned Consumer Information Center for its free publication entitled *Being an Executor* for further resources.

☐   I have made a will.

My will is kept_____

Person who prepared my will_____

Witnesses of my will_____

_____

Executor named in my will_____

Person I have named as guardian of minor children (if applicable):

_____

☐   I have not made a will.

Durable Power of Attorney for Financial Management

Planning in advance for the management of financial resources in the event of serious illness is an important consideration that everyone faces. The document known as a durable power of attorney for financial management allows you to designate another person (your "agent") to manage your financial affairs during your lifetime in the event you become physically or mentally incapacitated. (The term "durable" means that the document continues in effect even after you become incompetent.)

As with the durable power of attorney for health care (see pages 52–55), you decide exactly how much authority to give to your agent. Typically, most people give their agent a wide range of powers so that the agent may do things like pay bills, cash checks, make bank deposits and withdrawals, and access safe-deposit boxes; or you may limit your agent's authority to one or two tasks. While most durable powers of attorney for financial management take effect immediately after they are signed and continue in force indefinitely, you may limit their effective dates as you see fit.

You may either consult a lawyer or prepare your own durable power of attorney for financial management. Some state statutes include a model form of the document that you may easily adapt to meet your own needs, and commercial forms of this document are generally available in places like office supply and drug stores. You should be aware, however, that while your duly executed power of attorney must be honored, several banks and other financial institutions will prefer that you also complete their preprinted power of attorney form if your agent is to handle transactions on your behalf with that particular bank. To avoid problems, it is wise to check with each financial institution where you have an account and learn of their preferences.

☐ I have considered whether or not I need a durable power of attorney for financial management.

☐ I have executed a durable power of attorney for financial management. My named agent is

_____

Name   *Address*   *Telephone*

☐ I have checked with the financial institutions where I have accounts, and have filled out any required forms.

☐ I have decided not to execute a durable power of attorney for financial management.

Medical Treatment: Advance Directives

As a competent adult, you have the right to make decisions about your health care, and this right is not extinguished or lost when you become unable to make your own decisions. You have the right to execute "advance directives," written statements about the medical decisions you want made when you can no longer make them for yourself. Federal law requires that you be informed when you are admitted to a health care facility of your right to make advance directives. Hospitals in your area will likely have printed information available regarding advance directives in general. The Catholic Health Association of the United States also produces general material on advance directives: 4455 Woodson Road, St. Louis MO 63134-3797; (314) 253-3458; fax (314) 427-0029; www.chausa.org.

Two of the most commonly used advance directives are the durable power of attorney for health care and the living will. In addition, some states have recognized mental health treatment preference declarations. Each of these is discussed below.

When drafting your power of attorney for health care and your living will, you will need to know your mind regarding the provision of life-sustaining treatments. Catholic moral teaching allows for the discontinuation of medical treatments that are "burdensome, dangerous, extraordinary, or disproportionate to the expected outcome" (*Catechism of the Catholic Church*, 2278), as long as the ordinary or normal care due to a sick person in similar cases continues uninterrupted (#2279). You might find it helpful to discuss the moral issues surrounding medical care, death and dying with your pastor or other minister. More information is available from the National Conference of Catholic Bishops/United States Catholic Conference, 3211 4th Street NE, Washington DC 20017-1194; (202) 541-3000; www.nccbuscc.org/prolife/issues.

It is entirely your right to choose whether or not to execute any advance directive, but regardless of your decision, consider the value of at least discussing your wishes regarding your health care with family members or close personal friends, as appropriate. Consider also communicating your wishes to your physician, and taking an active and informed role in choosing treatment options and designing a health care plan.

If you do choose to execute one or more advance directives, be aware that such directives do little on their own. Your physician should know of their existence, and should be provided with a copy. The agent and any successor agent you name in a power of attorney should likewise know of your wishes and be given a copy. Advance directives that are signed and then put in a safe-deposit box and never discussed or distributed are worthless. Think of advance directives as more than an end in themselves. Use them as opportunities for communication with your physician and with other people you consider important to your health care decision-making. The real value of executing advance directives lies more in their potential to encourage honest communication with your health care providers and loved ones, and your informed participation in decisions affecting your health care, than in simply completing legal formalities.

DURABLE POWER OF ATTORNEY FOR HEALTH CARE • The document known as the durable power of attorney for health care allows you to designate a person (your "agent") to whom you give the power to make health care decisions for you, consistent with your wishes and values, in the event you become incompetent. The powers you give to your agent may be as broad or as narrow as you wish and specify in the document.

Almost every state has enacted legislation that authorizes durable powers of attorney for health care, and most state statutes include a standard form of the document, which is often made available at hospitals, nursing homes, pharmacies, office supply stores, senior centers, bar associations and the offices of health care professionals. With little effort you can obtain a copy of this form (one that conforms to your state's law), and can easily complete it yourself after taking some time to read through it, tailoring it to meet your own needs and wishes if desired. Standard forms for each state are available for a nominal fee from Choice in Dying, 1035 30th Street NW, Washington DC 20007; (800) 989-9455; or may be downloaded from www.choices.org.

The standard form generally gives your agent broad powers to make any and all health care decisions for you, including the authority to select a health care provider; admit or discharge you from any hospital; visit you in the hospital under the same right granted to a spouse or adult child; obtain access to your medical records and consent to their release; require, consent to or withdraw any type of medical treatment, including whether to withdraw artificially assisted nutrition and hydration and other life-sustaining measures; and make a disposition of your body for medical purposes, authorize an autopsy and direct the disposition of your remains.

Whether you use a standard form or create your own following the requirements of the applicable state law, you may always limit any power you give your agent, or may give only specific powers.

Your durable power of attorney for health care may also include a statement of your wishes regarding particular medical treatments (such as surgery, cardiopulmonary resuscitation, ventilation, intubation, blood transfusions, chemotherapy, medication and amputation). You also may specify your wishes regarding what measures should or should not be taken in the event you have a terminal illness and have become unable to communicate your wishes.

You may designate a successor agent (or successor agents, although only one may act in your name at any time) to act if the named agent is unable, unwilling or unavailable to serve when needed. No agent is under any duty to act or to exercise any power you have given them simply because they are named as your agent, and it is helpful to name a successor agent.

In some states, you must at least inform your physician of the existence of your durable power of attorney for health care. In any case, you would probably find it helpful to discuss the contents of your power of attorney with your physician, your agent and your successor agent and to provide each of them with a photocopy of your completed form. In many cases you will also find it beneficial to discuss your wishes and the contents of your power of attorney with others as well, such as close friends and family members.

☐ I have executed a durable power of attorney for health care.
The original form is kept_____
My named agent is

_____
Name   *Address*   *Telephone*

☐ I have named a successor agent.
My successor agent is

_____
Name   *Address*   *Telephone*

☐   I have informed my physician of the existence and contents of my durable power of attorney for health care, and have provided a copy to my physician's office for inclusion in my medical records.

_____
Name of physician   *Address*   *Telephone*

☐   I have discussed my wishes regarding my medical care with my agent and any successor agent, and have provided them with a copy of my durable power of attorney for health care.

☐   I have not executed a durable power of attorney for health care.

LIVING WILL • The living will is a document in which you make a declaration of your health care wishes in the event that you have a terminal illness or irreversible condition and are unable to communicate your health care decisions. As a general rule, a living will directs that if death is imminent, medical procedures that serve only to prolong the dying process are not to be used. Procedures that ease pain and those that maintain the comfort and dignity of the person are not considered death-delaying procedures.

Most states have enacted legislation recognizing living wills, and many of these state laws provide simple forms that you may use to create your own living will. Usually, in addition to bearing your own signature, living wills must be witnessed by two individuals 18 years of age or older who are not related to you by blood or marriage, not entitled to inherit from you, not financially responsible for your health care, and not your physician. Under most living will laws, one or two physicians must certify, in writing, that the patient is terminally ill before the living will goes into effect. It is important that you follow your state's regulations for living wills, as some requirements vary from state to state, such as the need to have the living will notarized or periodically renewed. Choice in Dying offers living will declarations for each state: 1035 30th Street NW, Washington DC 20007; (800) 989-9455; www.choices.org.

As with the durable power of attorney for health care, it is most helpful to provide your physician with a copy of your living will well in advance of any immediate need. In most cases, it is also beneficial to give copies to your family members and close friends, and to discuss the contents with them. The original should be kept in a secure, but known and easily accessible place.

It is important to remember that by its nature the living will deals only with your wishes to discontinue medical procedures that serve only to prolong the dying process. The living will does not offer any guidance except in situations dealing with death-delaying procedures. So, while the living will provides some benefit, it is wise to have a durable power of attorney for health care that names your agent for the purpose of making all health care decisions (including routine, day-to-day decisions) on your behalf when you are incompetent to do so, but not necessarily terminally ill.

☐　I have executed a living will.

　　The original form is kept_____

☐　I have informed my physician of the existence and contents of my living will, and have provided a copy to my physician's office for inclusion in my medical records.

_____

Name of physician　　　　　　　　　*Address*　　　　　　　*Telephone*

☐   I have informed my family members of the existence and contents of my living will, and have provided at least one family member or close personal friend with a copy of my living will.

_____

Name of person   *Address*   *Telephone*

☐   I have not executed a living will.

MENTAL HEALTH TREATMENT PREFERENCE DECLARATION • Through a durable power of attorney for health care you designate an agent to make decisions on your behalf regarding treatment of your physical and mental condition when you are incompetent to do so. While your physical health is in many cases the first thing you think of when working on a power of attorney for health care, treatment for a condition that affects your mental health is also a subject that is covered by your health care power of attorney. It is important not to neglect the mental health treatment component of your power of attorney.

You are always able to limit and direct the decision-making power you give your agent in your health care power of attorney, whether the issue involves your physical or mental health. You may, for example, instruct your agent to refuse certain mental health treatments that you consider unacceptable, such as psychosurgery or electroconvulsive therapy. Some states, however, specifically prohibit your agent from performing some or all of the following: admitting you to a mental health facility; consenting to psychosurgery; consenting to electroconvulsive treatment; consenting to treatment with psychotropic medicines. Some states have enacted separate laws that allow you to execute a mental health treatment preference declaration in which you state your wishes regarding such things as electroconvulsive treatment or psychotropic medication.

When thinking about your health care advance directives, it is important to consider your mental as well as your physical health, and any particular mental health care concerns you may have. It is also important to learn of your state's laws in this regard by either reading carefully the language in your durable power of attorney for health care, or by consulting your physician or attorney.

☐ I have learned of my state's laws regarding advance directives and mental health care.

☐ I have thought about my wishes concerning my mental health treatment, and have taken the necessary steps (following my state's laws) to make my wishes known to my physician and to my health care agent.

No Advance Directives?

You have the right not to execute any advance directives regarding your medical treatment in the event you are no longer able to communicate your wishes. But if you have not executed an advance directive, decisions regarding your health care will have to be made by someone else — someone who might not be the person you would have chosen.

The laws of many states provide that if you are not able to make your own health care decisions, and in the absence of an advance directive, a "health care surrogate" or "proxy" may be chosen to make your health care decisions for you. Typically, this health care surrogate or proxy will be one of the following persons, chosen in order of priority: spouse, an adult child, a parent, an adult brother or sister, a grandparent or adult grandchild or other adult relative, a close friend, or the guardian of the estate. A minority of states insert other persons in various positions of priority into this basic listing (for example, a member of the clergy known to you, a long-term domestic partner), and your state's law should be consulted for more information.

The chosen surrogate or proxy is to make health care decisions for you based on whatever he or she knows of your wishes; otherwise, the surrogate is to make decisions in accord with his or her determination of your best interests. It is helpful, then, even if you choose not to execute any advance directive, to discuss your thoughts and desires regarding your health care, as well as some of your personal, philosophical, religious or moral beliefs, with at least some of those persons likely to be chosen to act as your health care surrogate.

☐ I have chosen not to execute any advance directive regarding my health care.

☐ I have thought about my own wishes concerning my medical treatment in the event I become incompetent to communicate my desires.

☐ I have spoken of my wishes with the following likely candidates to be chosen to act as my health care surrogate or proxy.

_____

_____

_____

Donation of Organs and Body

Some persons choose to donate their usable organs to "organ banks" or their bodies for medical research. Catholic tradition supports such decisions. Pope Pius XII, speaking in 1956, said:

> A person may will to dispose of one's body and to destine it to ends that
> are useful, morally irreproachable, and even noble, among them the desire
> to aid the sick and suffering. One may make a decision of this nature
> with respect to one's own body with full realization of the reverence which
> is due it. . . . This decision should not be condemned but positively justified.

Arrangements for organ donations and donation of the body should be
made in advance. When death occurs, time is of the essence for useful
donation of organs. A donor card, which can be carried in one's wallet, aids
in fulfilling your wishes in this regard. Many states now have a place on
the back of a driver's license where one can indicate specific organs or the
entire body for donation.

It is important to discuss these intentions with family members,
friends, and if applicable, the person you named as your agent in your power
of attorney for health care. Even though a donor card has been signed,
doctors usually will not remove organs without the consent of the family
or health care agent.

☐   I have made the following arrangements for organ donation:

_____

_____

_____

_____

_____

_____

Financial Information

Stewardship is an attitude of responsibility to God and to one another for the material goods at our disposal. Such stewardship should be our perspective in approaching the following material. Regardless of how few or how many are our possessions, we have a responsibility to use these goods wisely. The careful answering of the items on the following pages is an exercise in stewardship.

Insurance and Death Benefits Information

Life insurance policies:

Company	Policy number	Agent's telephone

Other death benefits (credit union insurance, unions, organizations, employer insurance, social security benefits, veterans' benefits):

_____

_____

_____

_____

_____

For information regarding Social Security benefits, call (800) 772-1213; for information regarding veterans' benefits, call (800) 827-1000 or your local Office of Veterans Affairs. Note that in both cases, claims must be filed to receive available benefits.

Pension Benefits for Survivors

_____

_____

_____

_____

Bank, Savings and Loan, and Credit Union Accounts

Institution	Type of account	Account number

Real Estate

Location   *Mortgage held by / Location of deed*

_____

_____

_____

_____

Mutual Funds, Stocks and Bonds

Name   *Location of certificates*

_____

_____

_____

_____

_____

_____

Brokers, addresses and account numbers

_____

_____

_____

_____

Safe-Deposit Boxes

Location   *Box number*   *Location of key*

_____

_____

_____

_____

A Suggestion

After you complete working in this book, tell someone you trust about it. You may wish to discuss what you have written and what preparations you have made to be certain that it is clear. Tell the person where you will keep this book so that it will be readily available. You might choose to use the form on the following page to record this information. The page can then be removed from the book and given to the person to whom it is addressed.

This is my signature:_____

Date:_____

Date:_____

Dear_____:

As we have previously discussed, I have used the book *Now and at the Hour of Our Death* to record my preparations and desires regarding my medical treatment, finances, death and funeral.

I keep the book in the following place:

_____

_____

At the time of my death, I ask that you use the information in this book to the extent possible.

With gratitude,

_____

Signature